BRITANNICA BEGINNER BIOS

ALEXANDER HAMILTON

AMERICA'S FIRST TREASURY SECRETARY

SUSANNA KELLER

Britannica Educational Publishing
IN ASSOCIATION WITH
ROSEN EDUCATIONAL SERVICES

Published in 2018 by Britannica Educational Publishing (a trademark of Encyclopædia Britannica, Inc.) in association with The Rosen Publishing Group, Inc.
29 East 21st Street, New York, NY 10010

Distributed exclusively by Rosen Publishing.
To see additional Britannica Educational Publishing titles, go to rosenpublishing.com.

First Edition

Britannica Educational Publishing
J.E. Luebering: Executive Director, Core Editorial
Mary Rose McCudden: Editor, Britannica Student Encyclopedia

Rosen Publishing
Kathy Kuhtz Campbell: Editor
Nelson Sá: Art Director
Brian Garvey: Series Designer
Ellina Litmanovich: Book Layout
Cindy Reiman: Photography Manager
Bruce Donnola: Photo Researcher

Library of Congress Cataloging-in-Publication Data

Names: Keller, Susanna, author.
Title: Alexander Hamilton: America's first Treasury secretary / Susanna Keller.
Description: New York: Britannica Educational Services in Association with Rosen Publishing, 2018. | Series: Britannica beginner bios | Includes bibliographical references and index. | Audience: Grades 1–4.
Identifiers: LCCN 2017015312| ISBN 9781680488098 (library bound: alk. paper) | ISBN 9781680488081 (pbk.: alk. paper) | ISBN 9781538300213 (6 pack: alk. paper)
Subjects: LCSH: Hamilton, Alexander, 1757–1804—Juvenile literature. | Statesmen—United States—Biography—Juvenile literature. | United States—Politics and government—1783–1809—Juvenile literature.
Classification: LCC E302.6.H2 K4523 2017 | DDC 973.4092 [B]—dc23
LC record available at https://lccn.loc.gov/2017015312

Manufactured in the United States of America

Photo credits: Cover, pp. 1, 17 FPG/The Image Bank/Getty Images; p. 4 Frost & Reed, Ltd./Library of Congress, Washington, DC (LC-DIG-pga-03160); p. 5 Museum of the City of New York, USA/Bridgeman Images; p. 6 GraphicaArtis/Archive Photos/Getty Images; pp. 8, 9 Library of Congress Prints and Photographs Division; p. 11 Universal History Archive/Universal Images Group/Getty Images; p. 13 Stock Montage/Archive Photos/Getty Images; p. 15 The Federalist (vol. 1) J and A M'Lean, publisher, New York, 1788, from Rare Books and Special Collections Division in Madison's Treasures/Library of Congress, Washington, DC; p. 16 Library of Congress, Washington, DC (neg. no. LC-USZ62-3775); p. 18 Peter Newark American Pictures/Bridgeman Images; p. 19 FPG/Archive Photos/Getty Images; p. 20 U.S. Diplomacy Center; p. 21 MPI/Archive Photos/Getty Images; pp. 24, 26 Encyclopædia Britannica; p. 27 Bettmann/Getty Images; p. 28 Theo Wargo /WireImage/Getty Images.

CONTENTS

CHAPTER ONE

MEET ALEXANDER HAMILTON

The United States government was founded more than 240 years ago by a group of men who worked together but didn't always agree about what a government should do. This group is called the Founding Fathers. Alexander Hamilton was one of the youngest and brightest of the Founding Fathers.

Unlike most of the other founders, Hamilton was not born in one of the thirteen colonies that broke away from Great Britain to form the United States in 1776.

Alexander Hamilton was one of the Founding Fathers of the United States. He helped design the nation's government.

Soon after arriving in the colonies, Hamilton got caught up in their fight for independence. He joined a New York artillery company to fight against the British.

He was born in the West Indies. The West Indies are a chain of islands in the Caribbean Sea that extend from Florida to South America. Hamilton **IMMIGRATED** as a teenager, moving first to New Jersey and then to New York to get an education. The American Revolution broke out soon after Hamilton arrived. He enthusiastically joined the fight to win his new home its freedom from the British.

After the war, Hamilton was named the first secretary of the treasury. The treasury is the government department that collects taxes, borrows money for the government, and deals

Vocabulary

A person who IMMIGRATED moved to a new country to live there.

Quick Fact

The first political parties in the United States were the Federalist Party and the Republican Party (later called the Democratic-Republican Party). The parties that control the government today are the Democratic Party and the Republican Party.

Hamilton (*foreground, seated, wearing black*) joins in the signing of the US Constitution in 1787. After the United States won the American Revolution, the Founding Fathers needed to set up a lasting government for the new nation.

with other matters relating to money. Hamilton worked to create a strong national government. However, others were worried that the national government was too strong. These disagreements led the early leaders of the country to create two political parties. Hamilton led the Federalist Party.

CHAPTER TWO

A SMART YOUNG MAN

Alexander Hamilton was born on January 11, in about 1755, on the island of Nevis, in the British West Indies. His mother was Rachel Fawcett Lavine, the daughter of a French doctor. His father, James Hamilton, was a trader and the son of a Scottish nobleman. Alexander's parents weren't married, and the family was poor. These facts made some people look down on them. Alexander had a difficult childhood. The family moved to the nearby island of St. Croix in 1765, and James abandoned the family soon after. Rachel supported Alexander and his brother, James, by setting up a small shop, but she died in 1768.

Alexander Hamilton was born in this house on the island of Nevis.

Though still a boy, Alexander supported himself by working as a **CLERK**. He was good at his job but dreamed of moving on to greater things. Alexander learned quickly and loved reading. As a teenager, he wrote several pieces that were published, or printed, in a local newspaper. His intelligence impressed many of the island's leading citizens, who set up a

Quick Fact

For many years historians thought Hamilton was born in 1757, but research now suggests he was probably born two years earlier.

This small watercolor-and-ink portrait of Hamilton was made when he was about fifteen years old.

fund, a special sum of money, to pay for his education. Many people—including his friends, relatives, and employers—contributed.

Hamilton did not receive much formal education in the West Indies. The fund raised by his friends and family allowed him to move away to improve his education. He attended Elizabethtown Academy in what is now Elizabeth, New Jersey. Before long he was starting classes as a student at King's College (now Columbia University) in New York, New York.

Vocabulary

A **CLERK** keeps records and accounts.

Hamilton was a good student. However, his studies were interrupted by growing protests against Great Britain. At the time, Great Britain controlled New York and the other colonies. Many people in the colonies were unhappy about the way the British treated them. Hamilton spoke out in defense of the Boston Tea Party. In that incident, a group of colonists destroyed tea on ships in Boston, Massachusetts. They were protesting a tax that the British had imposed on tea. Hamilton wrote **PAMPHLETS** criticizing British policies and arguing for colonists to stop trading goods with Britain.

Hamilton joined a New York artillery company and, in 1776, became a captain. He was introduced to George Washington. The American commander in chief liked the young officer. From 1777 to 1781 Hamilton served on Washington's staff as a lieutenant colonel.

Vocabulary

PAMPHLETS are short printed publications with no hard covers.

Because Hamilton spoke French, he worked closely with the French generals and admirals (high-ranking navy officers) who fought on the colonists' side.

While in the military, Hamilton met and fell in love with Elizabeth Schuyler. She was the daughter of an American general and a member of one of New York's most respected families. The couple married in 1780.

Hamilton left his position as Washington's aide in 1781. He wanted to take a more active part in fighting the war. Washington put him in charge of a battalion, and Hamilton was part of the siege that forced the British army to surrender at Yorktown, Virginia.

General George Washington led the American colonists to victory in the American Revolution. Hamilton served on Washington's staff from 1777 to 1781.

CHAPTER THREE

FIGHTING FOR FEDERALISM

By November 1781, the war was basically over. Hamilton moved to Albany, New York, to study law. He passed the exam to become a lawyer in July 1782. The next year he began practicing law in New York City.

While serving as Washington's aide, Hamilton had come to believe that the United States needed a strong central government. After the war, he pushed for writing a new constitution to replace the weak Articles of Confederation. The Articles were America's first constitution. They were adopted in 1781. Hamilton was one of several leaders who realized that

The gathering that produced the US Constitution is now known as the Constitutional Convention. Hamilton and the others at the convention met at Independence Hall in Philadelphia.

there were problems with the Articles. In 1787 people met in Philadelphia, Pennsylvania, to change them. They soon wrote a completely new document—the

Vocabulary

DELEGATES are people sent with the power to act for others.

US Constitution. Hamilton was one of three **DELEGATES** sent to this meeting by the state of New York.

Hamilton worked hard to get others to join him in support of the new Constitution. With James Madison and John Jay, he wrote a series of essays to explain the Constitution to the public. They were signed "Publius" and would later come to be known as the Federalist papers. The series of eighty-five essays was published between 1787 and 1788.

Quick Fact

Seventy-seven of the Federalist essays were published in book form as *The Federalist* in 1788.

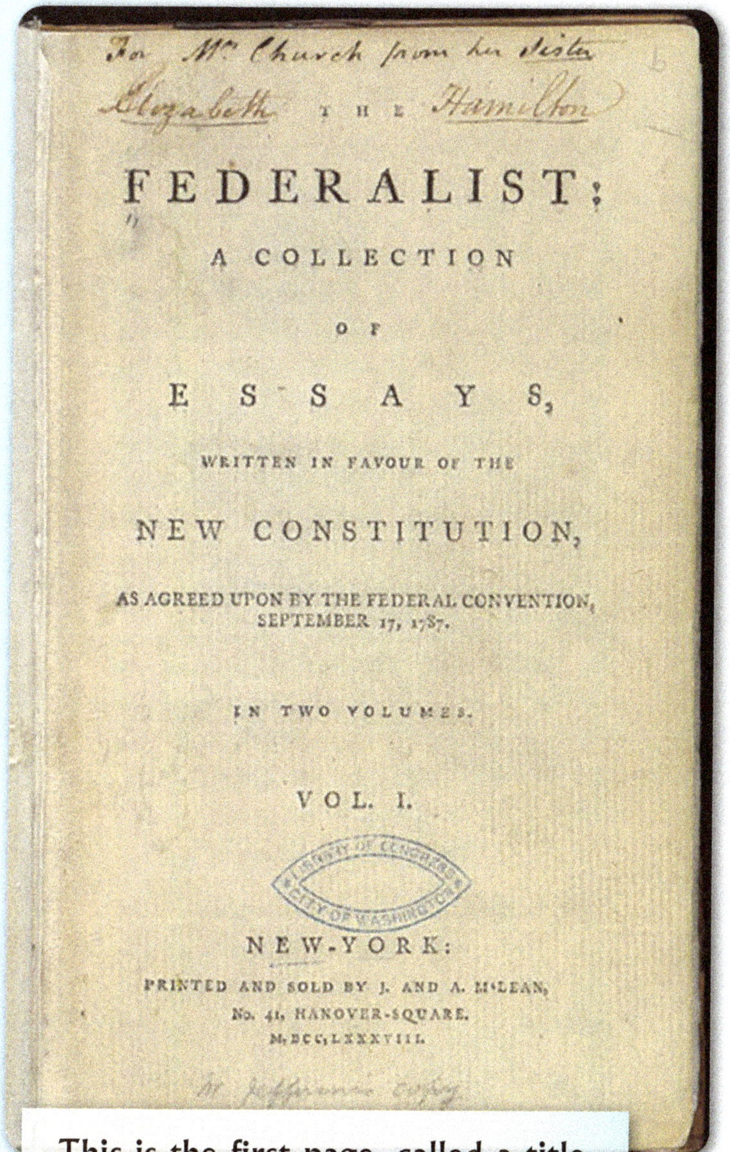

For Mrs Church from her Sister Elizabeth Hamilton

THE

FEDERALIST:

A COLLECTION

OF

ESSAYS,

WRITTEN IN FAVOUR OF THE

NEW CONSTITUTION,

AS AGREED UPON BY THE FEDERAL CONVENTION, SEPTEMBER 17, 1787.

IN TWO VOLUMES.

VOL. I.

NEW-YORK:

PRINTED AND SOLD BY J. AND A. M'LEAN,
No. 41, HANOVER-SQUARE.
M,DCC,LXXXVIII.

This is the first page, called a title page, of *The Federalist*, the book version of the Federalist papers that was published in 1788.

The essays defended the federal system of government that the Constitution set up. In a federal system the national government and the state governments share power. People who supported the federal system were called Federalists. Other people feared that the new national government would be too strong. They were called Anti-Federalists. Anti-Federalists were

Virginia's Patrick Henry (*right*) was a leading Anti-Federalist. His objection to ratifying the Constitution was one reason the Bill of Rights was added to it.

powerful in New York. To get the people of New York to **RATIFY** the Constitution, Hamilton, Jay, and Madison published the essays in New York newspapers.

The Federalist papers argued that the new federal government would not be too strong. They explained how the national government would share power with the states. They also explained that the Constitution divided

Vocabulary

To **RATIFY** something is to legally or officially approve it.

Hamilton made well-reasoned arguments in support of the Constitution. He also described how the federal government would share power with the states.

the power of the federal government into three branches—the legislative, executive, and judicial branches. A system of checks and balances would keep any of the branches from becoming too powerful.

These essays not only helped win New York's ratification but also had a major influence throughout the country. Scholars still recommend them to anyone who wants to understand the Constitution.

CHAPTER FOUR

SECRETARY OF THE TREASURY

Washington's first inauguration, or swearing in as president, took place on April 30, 1789, in New York City. Hamilton (*second from left*) attended the inauguration.

On April 30, 1789, George Washington was sworn in as the first US president. One of his first tasks was to pick his **CABINET**. He chose Hamilton to be the first secretary of the treasury.

Along with a secretary of the treasury, Washington's cabinet included a secretary of state, a secretary of war, and an attorney general.

Hamilton faced many challenges in his new job. One of the biggest challenges was dealing with the debts that had built up during the American Revolution. Wars are expensive, and the US government had borrowed money to pay for the revolution. Hamilton put measures in place to make sure that the United States would pay back its debts. He recommended that the federal government take on the debts that the individual states had accumulated during the Revolution, too. To raise the

Vocabulary

A CABINET is a group of advisers to the political head of a government.

Thomas Jefferson served as Washington's secretary of state. Unlike Hamilton, Jefferson did not think the country should have a national bank.

money to repay these debts, Hamilton proposed new taxes. However, many people in Congress opposed the plan. Hamilton then struck a bargain with Thomas Jefferson, a leading statesman from Virginia. Even though Jefferson opposed a strong federal government, he agreed to get other Southerners to support Hamilton's plan. In exchange, Hamilton supported establishing the nation's new capital close to Virginia, on the banks of the Potomac River (in what is now Washington, DC).

Hamilton and Jefferson also disagreed over whether the United States should have a national bank. Hamilton was for a national bank, while Jefferson was against it. Hamilton won, and the Bank of the United States was founded in 1791. The Bank of the United States was successful in controlling the money supply in the country. At the time, the United States was growing fast. Many people wanted to borrow money from banks to expand businesses. Their growing businesses would bring in more money. This gain would allow them to pay back the banks. The in-

The first Bank of the United States lasted from 1791 to 1811. Its main branch was this building in Philadelphia.

Vocabulary

Things in CIRCULATION pass from person to person or place to place.

crease in bank loans caused more money to be in **CIRCULATION**. Too much available currency could cause prices to rise. The Bank of the United States decided how much currency should be available. It also set interest rates, which tell how much it costs to borrow money. These decisions affected the country's prices and level of employment.

Hamilton and Jefferson became the leaders of the first organized political parties in the United States. Hamilton led the Federalist Party, and Jefferson led the Republican Party. Jefferson opposed Hamilton's efforts to strengthen the federal government. He believed the states should have more power. The two men also had different opinions on foreign affairs. Hamilton was pro-British, while Jefferson favored

Quick Fact

Hamilton disliked political parties. He believed they led to disorder and instability. However, he needed organized political support to accomplish his goals.

revolutionary France. Hamilton even went so far as to interfere with Jefferson's duties as Washington's secretary of state. Jefferson was in charge of dealing with foreign countries. Hamilton sometimes tried to involve himself with international matters, which upset Jefferson.

CHAPTER FIVE

A LASTING LEGACY

Hamilton left the cabinet in 1795, but George Washington continued to ask him for advice on government matters. When Washington left office, Hamilton helped write his Farewell Address. The address was printed in a Philadelphia newspaper. This letter to his fellow citizens offered Washington's advice,

This painting shows Hamilton (*right*) helping President Washington write his now-famous Farewell Address.

Quick Fact

In 1801, Hamilton helped found a newspaper, the *New York Evening Post*. The paper promoted Federalist ideas.

including criticism of political parties and a warning against getting too involved in international matters.

Even after leaving Washington's cabinet, Jefferson and Hamilton continued to disagree. Hamilton's dislike of statesman Aaron Burr proved even stronger than his objections to Jefferson, though. Jefferson ran for the presidency in the election of 1800, with Burr as his running mate. Jefferson and Burr received an equal number of votes in the electoral college. When individuals cast their vote for a candidate in a general election for the presidency, they actually vote for a slate of electors. The electors then vote for the president. Under the procedures of the time, the electors cast their votes for individual candidates. Whoever got the most votes would be president. The person with the second most votes would be vice president. In 1800, the House of Representatives had to break the tie and decide which candidate would become president. Hamilton distrusted Burr. He also knew that the voters wanted Jefferson to be president. So he temporarily set aside his feud with Jefferson and convinced most of the Federalists to vote for Jefferson instead of Burr.

In 1804, Hamilton supported Burr's opponent in the election for governor of New York. Burr was angry with

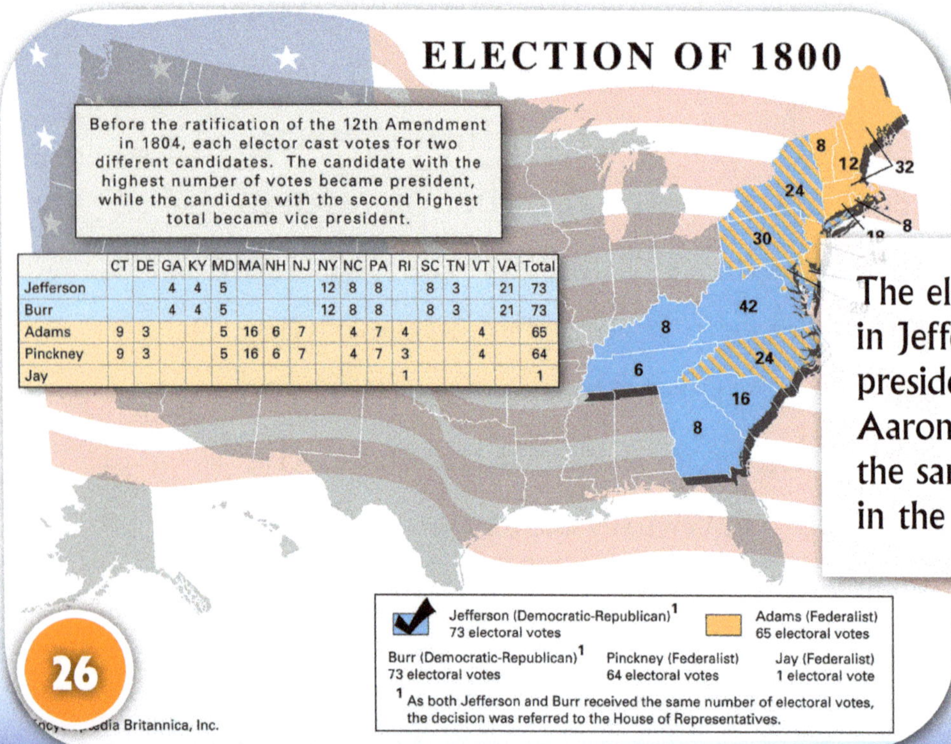

	CT	DE	GA	KY	MD	MA	NH	NJ	NY	NC	PA	RI	SC	TN	VT	VA	Total
Jefferson			4	4	5				12	8	8		8	3		21	73
Burr			4	4	5				12	8	8		8	3		21	73
Adams	9	3			5	16	6	7		4	7	4			4		65
Pinckney	9	3			5	16	6	7		4	7	3			4		64
Jay												1					1

The election of 1800 resulted in Jefferson becoming president, although he and Aaron Burr both received the same number of votes in the electoral college.

Hamilton and Burr fought their tragic duel in Weehawken, New Jersey, which is across the Hudson River from New York City.

Hamilton. He challenged Hamilton to a duel. A duel is an armed fight between two people, usually over a question of honor. Burr shot Hamilton on July 11, 1804. Hamilton died the next day.

Hamilton was a man both of action and of ideas. He was ambitious, hardworking, practical, and highly intelligent. Though he had a difficult childhood and a family others looked down on, he became very successful. Like many immigrants, he made major contributions to the United States. Hamilton was an early backer of national unity. He believed in an indivisible country in

Quick Fact

Hamilton had eight children. His oldest son, Philip, was killed in a duel at the age of nineteen, just a few years before his father's death.

Stars of the original version of *Hamilton* on Broadway included Leslie Odom Jr. (*left*) as Burr and writer Lin-Manuel Miranda (*right*) as Hamilton.

which the people would give their loyalty not to any state but to the nation. His writings on the proper role of government are still read and debated today. His life even inspired a hit musical on Broadway! In 2015, Lin-Manuel Miranda's *Hamilton* opened and became enormously popular.

TIMELINE

About 1755: Alexander Hamilton is born on the island of Nevis, in the West Indies, on January 11.

1765: Hamilton's family moves to the island of St. Croix. Soon after, his father abandons the family.

1768: Hamilton's mother dies.

1774: Hamilton begins his studies at King's College, in New York, New York.

1775: The American Revolution begins with the Battles of Lexington and Concord, in Massachusetts.

1776: In March, Hamilton becomes the captain of an artillery unit in the Continental Army.

On July 4, the Continental Congress adopts the Declaration of Independence.

1777: General George Washington appoints Hamilton to his staff.

1780: Hamilton marries Elizabeth Schuyler on December 14.

1781: Hamilton leads an assault at the Siege of Yorktown on October 14.

1782: His first child is born on January 22.

1787: Hamilton attends the Constitutional Convention in Philadelphia, Pennsylvania.

Hamilton, John Jay, and James Madison begin writing the Federalist papers.

1789: Washington picks Hamilton to be the first secretary of the treasury.

1790: Hamilton delivers a report to Congress calling for the establishment of a national bank.

1795: He steps down from his cabinet post.

1800: Hamilton supports Jefferson over Burr in the presidential election.

1801: The first issue of the *New York Evening Post* is published on November 16.

1804: Aaron Burr shoots Hamilton on July 11. Hamilton dies the next day.

GLOSSARY

ABANDON To completely give up or move away from something.

AMBITIOUS Having a desire to be successful, powerful, or famous.

ARTILLERY A branch of the army with large guns (such as cannons or rockets).

BATTALION A military unit composed of two or more smaller units.

COLONY A distant territory belonging to or under the control of a nation.

CONVINCE To make a person agree or believe by arguing or showing evidence.

CURRENCY Money that is in use.

DEBT Money that is owed to another person, group, or country.

DEPARTMENT A major administrative division of a government or business.

EMPLOYMENT Having a job; or the number of people in a country or other place who have jobs.

ESSAY A usually short written work giving a personal view or opinion on a subject.

EXECUTIVE BRANCH The branch of government in charge of making sure laws are carried out.

FEDERALISM A form of government in which power is distributed between a central authority and individual units.

INDIVISIBLE Impossible to divide or separate.

JUDICIAL BRANCH The branch of government that consists of the court system.

LEGISLATIVE BRANCH The branch of government in charge of passing laws.

POLICIES Courses of action chosen to guide people in making decisions.

PROCEDURES A series of steps followed in a regular definite order.

REPRESENTATIVE A person who represents, or acts or speaks for, others, especially in government.

BOOKS

Brown, Don. *Aaron and Alexander: The Most Famous Duel in American History*. New York, NY: Roaring Brook Press, 2015.

Kanefield, Teri. *Alexander Hamilton: The Making of America*. New York, NY: Abrams Books for Young Readers, 2017.

Kelley, K. C. *Alexander Hamilton: American Hero*. New York, NY: Children's Press, 2017.

Rice, Dona Herweck. *Alexander Hamilton's New York City*. Huntington Beach, CA: Teacher Created Materials, 2017.

Shea, Therese. *Alexander Hamilton: Founding Father and Treasury Secretary*. New York, NY: Enslow Publishing, 2018.

WEBSITES

Because of the changing nature of internet links, Rosen Publishing has developed an online list of websites related to the subject of this book. This site is updated regularly. Please use this link to access the list:

http://www.rosenlinks.com/BBB/Hamilton

INDEX